GAS SMOKER COOKBOOK

ULTIMATE COOKBOOK FOR MAKING GREAT BARBECUE, COMPLETE GUIDE FOR SMOKING MEAT, FISH, GAME AND VEGETABLES

PAUL RODGERS

TABLE OF CONTENTS

INTRODUCTION

What is better than smelling the fragrant smoke of your favourite meat cuts while the birds are singing in the early morning of a Sunday? Smoke is by far, one of the most cherished cooking techniques all over the world not only for its versatile health benefits, but also for the social role it plays in uniting the families and creating an adorable ambiance with the appetizing and inviting odours it offers.

Smoking food is the process of using natural smoke in order to give as much flavour as possible to your favourite dishes and portions of meat and no matter which type of meat you use; smoking food can completely give you the great flavour you are looking for and even more.

And if you wonder what is smoking exactly, let me tell you that this is a slow cooking technique that helps cook food indirectly over a source of fire and this can only be done with the help of a smoker. For instance a smoker is generally designed for outdoor uses. And the use of smoking techniques can be described as one of the oldest methods of cooking meat and of preserving it for a long time.

Smoking meats is indeed known for being one of the oldest methods used for preserving meats as well as sausages and even vegetables. And this cooking technique stemmed from the need to preserve foods in different climatic conditions. Indeed, the climatic changes and differences were significant in developing the smoke cooking technique and in developing various smoking brands.

And while some people prefer using smoking on wood, many other are showing interest more and more in using more practical smokers like Gas smokers. Gas smoker is a revolutionary smoking technique that comes to challenge conventional smokers like wood smokers. Not only gas smokers are easy to clean and to use, but it is also very practical. For instance, gas smokers can be used outdoors, even in rainy weather, in windy weather in winter or summer.

The entire smoking process is very simple once you use a gas smoker; all you need to do is to cook food until it reaches the perfect temperature. And using a Gas smoker won't deprive you from using your favourite wood chops like apple, cherry or lemon woodchips. And once food is in the smoker, cook until it reaches a safe temperature as determined with a food thermometer. The entire gas smoking process uses temperature that range from 65° F to about 250°F and you will be surprised that the food will be cooked to perfection with no so much effort. You are really going to like gas smokers if you try it.

CHAPTER 1: SMOKING MEAT

SMOKING MEAT BASIC TIPS

Mastering the art of smoking foods makes the objective of every cook around the world. And in order to be able to perfect the smoking foods; there are some basics and instructions each of us needs to follow in order to achieve it.

So now that you are ready to begin, start by lighting your smoker and get started, here are some tips that can help you enjoy the taste you are seeking:

1. Smoking food needs a low heat and keep it low for a few hours allowing the smoke to penetrate through the meats. Maintaining a consistent heat makes a key factor that can positively affect your smoking process and this process can be quite simple. You can use a chimney starter to get your coals to a temperature of about 250° F. And if you don't have a thermometer, the best way to determine the right temperature is to hold your hand on top of the coals.

    It is very simple; all you have to do is to pile the coals over the bottom; then add the smoking wood and put the meat onto the grill right into the opposite side of the coals you use. You can always add coals from time to time to maintain the same temperature.

2. **Smoking meat needs patience**

Smoking meat is a long process that needs a few hours. For instance, slow cooking meat through smoking it breaks down the meat into tender pieces and keeps its flavours and juiciness.

There are different types of meat, each type takes between about 5 to 7 hours to be perfectly smoked. Make sure not to peek at your ingredients while it is smoking, except for adding more coals to maintain a balanced temperature or to refill the water pan.

3. Decide whether you want the smoking process to be dry or wet:

The wet smoking process includes a pan filled with water and coals that can create a smoky atmosphere that will help moisturize the meat. You can also use a fruit juice or any other types of equipments to add extra favours. Wet smoking results in a flavourful bark that people will love.

4. Make sure to choose the right meat for you

Not all types of meat are suitable for smoking meat; turkey and chicken make a good meat choice; but since the smoking process takes a long time, the skin won't stand up. Besides, brining will help you through the process of smoking.

5. Using a rub is substantial in any smoking process

Making the rub is very important before smoking food and for a perfect rub you can combine about ½ cup of kosher salt with 1 tablespoon of lemon pepper, ½ cup of brown sugar, 1 tablespoon of black pepper, and about 2 teaspoons of chilli flakes; then Rub this mixture over the meat right before you start smoking.

6. Choose the right wood

In order to smoke meat properly you should carefully choose the wood you are going to use. For instance, apple wood will offer you a sweet and fruity smoke that goes very well with pork while using Hickory wood makes a perfect choice that you can use with red meat like ribs. You can use alder meat with poultry, fish and any type of white meat.

Pecan wood burns in a cooler way in comparison to other woods and makes a perfect choice to cook pork and brisket roasts. You can also use oak wood, cherry wood and other types of food according to the type of meat and the type of flavour you want to use.

7. The importance of brining in the process of smoking:

Brining any type of meat can keep it meat keeps it from drying out during the process of smoking food. The salt within the brine can make the used proteins more water absorbent. Indeed, when the sodium and the chloride ions get into the proteins tissue so that they can hold onto the moisture. It is recommended to soak the meat in the brine for about 10 to 12 hours right before smoking it.

GAS SMOKERS

Gas smokers make one of the most convenient smoking cookware that will save you from waking up 3am to tend fire. In this cookbook, you will find everything you have dreamt of from gas smoking tips, using guide, various delicious recipes and even more? So what are you waiting for to start your gas smoking experience?

Using Gas Smoker will allow both you and your family to enjoy a wide variety of recipes that range of smoked meats, veggies and different types of ingredients that you can cook both indoors and outdoors alike. And not only gas smoker is easy to use, but it needs a very minimal effort to get your dishes ready. And what is great about gas smoker is that it can offer you the same delicious taste conventional wood smokers grant you. Thus, you can impress your guests with a large array of sumptuous dishes that you can professionally make with simple utensils and cooking equipments.

Whether you want to serve your family smoked pork ribs, smoked salmon or beef jerky, this gas smoker cookbook makes the perfect choice for you; and if you want to know why, keep reading because this cookbook will answer all your questions. With this cookbook you can now cook everything you are dreaming of to perfection with no great effort. So all you need to do is to download get your own copy of this book right now and get ready to learn one of the most appealing smoke cooking techniques ever? With this Gas smoker Cookbook, you will get the opportunity to learn a large variety of International recipes from all over the world and you can start with:

- Spicy smoked chicken recipes
- Smoked baby back ribs
- Lemon garlic crab legs
- Smoked vegetables
- Smoked shrimp and more

GAS SMOKER DEFINITION AND ORIGINS

Making one of the oldest cooking methods in the entire world, smoking food emerged shortly after the development of cooking food with fire. And the use of smoking method attained unrivalled levels in no time before quickly spreading to reach many countries everywhere.

So what does smoking food stand for? And what are the origins of Smoke cooking? And the practice of smoking food has affected the culinary cultures of different cultures around the world, especially in North-western North America and in Scandinavia too. Not long after that, the production of smoked hams swept Europe. And although the production of smoked food witnessed a critical decline during the 20th century mainly because of the incredible popularity of food that uses chemical preservatives; it regained its popularity later and was classified as healthy food.

Indeed, smoking food is a technique that involves placing meat over racks in a specified chamber that is designed to contain all the smoke that emerges from burning wood. So smoking food usually uses steampipes in order to help provide the smoking machines with the heat it needs. And whatever type of smoking machine, the result is gorgeous, and the obtained smoked food is always unique, of flavourful and packed with nutrients.

In general, the temperatures of smokehouses vary from about 109°F to approximately 160° F. And usually, the whole process of smoking food takes a few hours to a few days to be perfectly smoked depending on the type of the used ingredients and meat. Usually, after the process of smoking food, the meat has to be rapidly chilled and cut; then wrapped to be prepared for retail and trading.

Beef Hams, sausages, pork, game meat, fish and seafood make some of the most popular American foods that are usually smoked. And with the evolution of the process of smoke cooking technique, you can now smoke different types of ingredients even cheeses, seeds, liver and nuts. And if we want to define the word smoking; it is a method of processing food for the purpose of preserving it or improving its flavour by excessively exposing ingredients to smoke mainly from burning wood. And the action of smoking foods leads to drying it thanks to the chemical compounds that are present in wood smoked.

But with the evolution of the culinary world, smoking machines have evolved from conventional and simple wood smokers to electric smokers and even gas smokers. And this cookbook focuses mainly on gas smokers. In fact, gas smokers make a top notch and revolutionary cookware that smokes foods without the need for a huge pile of wood logs and it only no more than a few equipments to start smoking food and the result can be amazing.

GAS SMOKER BENEFITS

Although Smoking foods is a cooking technique that needs patience, but the resulting dishes are worth trying mainly because of the great flavours and richness it gives to various ingredients. For instance, many people still wake up early to enjoy smoking their favourite foods and this is tradition that has always been cherished long time ago in different cultures when people used to smoke fish and meat by wrapping it into large leaves on top of outdoor open fire just like Indians used to do.

However, nowadays, with the advent of cooking appliances like stoves and smokers, smoking foods has become the trend of the century because it unites the family and greatly encourages communication and makes eating a pleasing experience to youngsters and elders alike. There are many types and brands of smokers and this book will be focusing on gas smokers.

Gas fuelled smokers are known for having many benefits and great qualities and unlike conventional smokers, gas smokers are known for their efficiency and for the versatility of this type of cookware. And here some of the most important advantages of using a Gas smoker:

1. Gas smokers can make smoking foods easier as you can use this type of smoker whatever weather whether in rainy or even windy weather without any risks. Besides, Gas smokers are safe to use by all people.
2. Unlike wood smokers, Gas smokers are easy-to use while camping and wherever you want, even in places where there are no wood logs at all. And what makes lighting Gas smokers easier is that fuel is available wherever you go. Besides, gas is available in every location you go to.
3. Gas smokers are used by people who love smoked foods and who want to try new smoking methods. But what makes gas smokers more useful than conventional brands of smokers is that Gas smokers are characterized by their mobility
4. Gas smokers are known for its high ability to produce clean heat, which makes smoking with gas smokers healthier to use in

comparison to conventional brands of smokers. And what is more exciting about Gas smokers is that you can still use your favourite wood chips like apple chips, chunks and hickory chips.

5. Many gas smokers are equipped with a smoking cast iron box that you can use to keep the coals or wood insulated inside it and thus you can rest assured that your Gas smoker is safe to use and very easy to prevent chips from burning quickly.

6. Some people love using all brands of smokers while many other people love building their own Smokers so that they can adjust it to their preferences. However, not all people are capable of building smokers, especially if it gas smoker. So it is advisable to buy gas smokers that are available in markets and there are some affordable gas smokers.

7. The Gas smokers that are available in markets are equipped with some adjustable dampers and this can help ensure a proper ventilation process. Besides, Gas smokers are also manufactured to the same style of ovens. Indeed, Gas smokers are designed with a full size door that can make smoking quicker.

8. Gas smokers are known for their durability. For instance, you can use Gas smokers for your entire life and even pass it to your children and grandchildren if you follow the necessary safeguards.

GAS SMOKER USE AND TIPS AND SAFEGUARDS

Most gas smokers are characterised by the same design and simple structure as well as use. Any gas smoker is connected to a propane tank or just a gas line and we can see this tank placed right onto the bottom. Most models of Gas smokers are also equipped with smaller lockers and you can a find a burner right into the bottom; the burner can be cast iron or brass.

Above the burner of every Gas smoker; we can find a tight shelf designed to place a pan for the wood over it. And above this pan, we can find a shelf for water pot. And above this shelf, we can find four shelves for food ingredients. The bottom vents of Gas smokers can't be adjusted in order to make sure that gas gets the oxygen it needs to smoker food properly.

At the top of every gas smoker, we can find a damper or two or a chimney. And to properly use the Gas Smoker, you should pay make sure to leave the top of the vent all the way open in order to prevent any soot from building up on top of the meat.

And now that you are aware of the different parts of a Gas smoker, you should know some basic tips that may help you master the use of this smoker perfectly and here are some of the most useful tips you can start with.

1. **Season your smoker:** The process of seasoning your smoker is very simple and all you have to do to start is to coat the inside of your Gas smoker with the help of a film of smoke residue. And this step will help protect your smoker and helps keep it in a good condition.

2. **Carefully and gently wash the outside and inside** of the Gas Smoker with a small quantity of warm water and with a little bit of detergent. Then rinse the smoker with clean water and leave it to dry later.

3. Fill the Wood chip box in your Gas smoker with pre-soaked wood chips of your choice; then light your smoker and set the level of gas to medium.

4. Be careful of using the water bowl

5. Once the Gas smoker is filled up with smoke; leave your gas smoker to season for about 30 minutes. You can also re-season the Gas smoker from time to time and you can do this at least once per year.

6. Before starting to use your Gas Smoker, make sure to gather all the utensils and equipments for great results.

7. By the end of the process of gas smoking food, it is recommended to use two kinds of thermometers so that you can check the inner temperature of the cooked meat and to check it for doneness and another thermometer to check the temperature of the smoker box.

8. While using your gas smoker, you should prepare a pair of BBQ tongs that can help you safely remove small pieces of meat from the Smoker.

9. You can also use a pair of long BBQ mitts to make sure you don't burn your forearms or hands.

10. Make sure to keep an aluminium foil close to you to. Indeed, it is also recommended to wrap the meat within aluminium foil and once the meat reaches the recommended temperature, remove the foil. So using an aluminium foil can prevent your food from burning. It is also recommended to line the wood chip box and the water pan with a foil before using it and this can make the cleaning process easier.

11. Soak the smoker wood chips in a bowl filled with water for about 20 minutes and doing this can improve the smoky flavour. Besides, soaking wood chips can give you a longer burning time. And once you start your Gas smoker, place it a ventilated area.

12. Fill the woodchip pan with your favourite woodchips; then place the pan in the bottom of your gas smoker.

13. Insert the water pan in your gas smoker and add in hot water or you can also use other liquids like wine or beer.

14. Make sure to insert clean cooking grills in your Gas smoker

15. Always keep in mind that dome meat may drip during the smoking process, so you should place the vegetables if you use any on top of the shelf aver the meat in order to eliminate any contamination danger.

CHAPTER 2: GAS SMOKER BEEF RECIPES

SMOKED BEEF BRISKET WITH BBQ SAUCE

(Prep time: 20 Minutes|Cook Time: 10 Hours| Servings: 6)

INGREDIENTS

- 4 Pounds of Beef brisket
- 3 Minced garlic cloves
- 1 Heap tablespoon of salt
- 1 Teaspoon of black pepper
- 1 ½ tablespoons of paprika
- ½ Teaspoon of Cayenne pepper
- ½ Teaspoon of ground thyme
- ½ Teaspoon of dried mustard
- 2 ½ cups of barbecue sauce

INSTRUCTIONS

1. Combine the salt with the garlic, the paprika, the cayenne pepper, the thyme and the dried mustard in a small bowl and mix very well
2. Coat the beef brisket with the prepped dry rub and add an amount of mustard
3. Cover the mustard with the mixture of the mustard and spices rub; then coat the beef very well with the mixture
4. Smoke the beef brisket with light fruit wood for about 4 hours; then continue cooking the beef brisket for 6 additional hours
5. Run the Gas smoker at a temperature of about 90° C (190°F)
6. In the last 2 and ½ hours; coat the beef brisket with the 1 ½ cups of BBQ Sauce.
7. Serve and enjoy the smoked beef brisket with the honey and the remaining quantity of BBQ sauce!

NUTRITION INFORMATION

Calories: 243, Fat: 15.7g, Carbohydrates: 0g, Dietary Fiber 0.3 g, Protein: 25.5g

SMOKED RIB EYE

(Prep time: 30 Minutes|Cook Time: 5 Hours| Servings: 4)

INGREDIENTS

FOR THE RIB

- 5 lbs of rib eye
- ¼ Cup of extra virgin olive oil
- 2 Tablespoons of coarse ground pepper
- 2 Tablespoons of kosher salt

TO PREPARE THE HERB PASTE

- 3 Garlic cloves
- 1 Tablespoon of fresh rosemary
- 1 Tablespoon of fresh thyme
- 1 Tablespoon of fresh sage
- ¼ Cup of extra virgin olive oil

INSTRUCTIONS

1. Start with the Herb Paste and to prepare it place all your ingredients in a food processor and pulse your ingredients for a couple or three times until you get a chunky paste
2. For the rib:
3. Preheat your Gas Smoker to a temperature of 225° F
4. Trim any excess of fat off of the meat; then rinse it with cold water and pat it dry.
5. Apply the olive oil; the salt and the pepper generously to rib eye and apply the paste on top of it
6. Place the rib eye on top of a shelf in your gas smoker with the side down
7. Fill the wood chip box with the pre-soaked apple chips
8. Smoke the rib eye for about 5 hours; then check the temperature of the meat with a thermometer
9. Remove the smoked meat from the gas smoker and let sit for about 20 minutes
10. Serve and enjoy your smoked rib eye!

NUTRITION INFORMATION

Calories: 207, Fat: 12g, Carbohydrates: 0.6g, Dietary Fiber 0.5 g, Protein: 24g

STUFFED BEEF ROLL

(Prep time: 15 Minutes|Cook Time: 4 Hours| Servings: 6)

INGREDIENTS

- 1 to 2 pounds of butterflied flank steak
- 1 Teaspoon of separated salt
- 1 Teaspoon of separated black pepper
- 1 Package of 10 ounces of chopped frozen spinach, thawed and very well-drained
- ½ Cup of chopped sun-dried tomatoes
- 2 Cups of grated mozzarella cheese
- 2 Tablespoons of extra virgin olive oil

INSTRUCTIONS

1. Preheat your gas smoker to a LOW temperature of 105 to 135°C (220-275°F)
2. Start by placing the butterflied steak on top of a cutting board.
3. Season the steak with about ½ teaspoon of salt and about ½ teaspoon of pepper
4. Spread the cheese over the steak; then
5. Top with the spinach and the sun-dried tomatoes and make sure to leave about 2 inches of border right on top side of the steak.
6. Start by tightly rolling the steak with the grain by going all the length of the roll
7. Tie the roll with a kitchen twine at intervals of about 1 inch each.
8. Brush the outside of roll with a small quantity of olive oil and season with about ½ teaspoon of salt and ½ teaspoon of pepper.
9. Place the rolled steak in a foil pack on top of a shelf in your gas smoker
10. Slowly smoke the rolled and stuffed beef for about 3 to 4 hours with the door of the gas smoker closed, always remember to keep the vent open
11. When the temperature of the meat roll indicates 135 to 140 degrees, add 150 l of juice marinade to the foil pack and let sit for about 10 minutes
12. Serve and enjoy your dish!

NUTRITION INFORMATION

Calories: 201, Fat: 11g, Carbohydrates: 0.4g, Dietary Fiber 0.3 g, Protein: 23g

JAPANESE-STYLE SMOKED STEAK
(Prep time: 30 Minutes|Cook Time: 5 Hours| Servings: 4)

INGREDIENTS

- 2 Pounds of grass-fed organic flank steak
- 1 and ½ cups of Full Sugar Coca-Cola™
- 1 Cup of organic Japanese shoyu
- 6 Minced garlic cloves
- 1 Pinch of grated ginger
- 1 Pinch of fresh ground white pepper

INSTRUCTIONS

1. Mix the Coke with the shoyu, the garlic and the ginger in a sealable Ziploc bag.
2. Add the trimmed flank steak and let marinate for an overnight. Soak about 15 chunks of mesquite wood into water for an overnight
3. Place the soaked mesquite chunks into the wood bottom of your gas smoker
4. Add the water to the pan box covered with aluminium foil; then turn on the heat
5. Place the flank steak over the rack in your gas smoker; then add the white pepper
6. Lock the lid of the gas smoker and smoke the beef meat for about 5 hours
7. Check the temperature of the meat with a thermometer and if the internal temperature indicates 160°F; the meat is done
8. You can add more wood chips and spray the meat with cider vinegar to keep the moisture
9. Remove the meat from the gas smoker and set aside for about 15 minutes under a foil cover
10. Slice the beef meat; then serve and enjoy its taste!

NUTRITION INFORMATION

Calories: 327.6, Fat: 14g, Carbohydrates: 13.8g, Dietary Fiber: 4.6 g, Protein: 39.5g

SMOKED BEEF BACK RIBS
(Prep time: 60 Minutes|Cook Time: 6 Hours| Servings: 6)

INGREDIENTS

- 2 Racks of baby back ribs
- ¼ Cup of packed light brown sugar
- 1 Tablespoon of chilli powder
- 1 Tablespoon of paprika
- 2 Teaspoons of ground cumin
- 1 Teaspoon of mustard powder
- 2 Tablespoons of Kosher salt
- 1 Halved lemon

- 1 Quartered apple
- 1 Cup of cider or apple juice
- 2 tablespoons of Worcestershire sauce
- 1 Tablespoon of apple cider vinegar
- 1 Tablespoon of vegetable oil, for brushing
- 8 to 10 cups of mesquite wood chips
- 1 Small bottle of spray

INSTRUCTIONS

1. Start by combining the brown sugar, the chilli powder, the paprika, the cumin, the mustard powder and the 2 tablespoons salt in a small bowl.
2. Rub the prepared ribs all over the beef cuts; then season with the spice mixture and lemon
3. Place the meat cuts in a resealable plastic bag; then cover and let refrigerate for about 2 hours or for an overnight.
4. Soak the wood chips into water for about 1 hour; then prepare the gas smoker
5. Fill the smoker box with one quarter of wood and apple chips
6. Just about 30 minutes before smoking the meat, remove the ribs from your refrigerator and set it aside for 5 minutes
7. Mix the apple juice with the Worcestershire sauce and the vinegar in a small bottle for spray and shake to mix the ingredients.
8. Preheat your gas smoker at a temperature of 135°F for about 10 minutes; then lightly brush the grates with vegetable oil
9. Place the beef ribs on the cooker side of the gas smoker shelf
10. Spray the ribs with the apple juice mixture and close the door of the gas smoker
11. Smoke the beef ribs for about 1 to 2 hours
12. Replenish your smoker box with another batch of apple wood chips.
13. Flip the beef ribs and spray with the apple juice mixture
14. Close the gas smoker and smoke the beef ribs for 1 additional hour and repeat the same process every hour until the ribs start getting darker; for about 2 to 3 hours

15. Remove the beef ribs from the gas smoker and let rest for about 5 minutes before slicing it
16. Serve and enjoy!

NUTRITION INFORMATION

Calories: 174, Fat: 10.7g, Carbohydrates: 0g, Dietary Fiber: 0.5 g, Protein: 25g

CHAPTER 3: GAS SMOKER PORK RECIPES

SMOKED PORK LOIN

(Prep time: 30 Minutes|Cook Time: 4 Hours| Servings: 5)

INGREDIENTS

- 4Cups of apple wood chips
- 1 Trimmed pork loin, trimmed
- 3 Tablespoons of canola oil
- 2Tablespoons of garlic powder
- 2Tablespoons of finely chopped dried rosemary
- ¼Cup of kosher salt
- ½ Cup of dry chopped roasted pistachios
- 1Cup of ground black peppercorns

INSTRUCTIONS

1. Load the Gas smoker box with the wood chips and preheat it for about 35 minutes.
2. The set the temperature to 235 degrees F
3. Pat the pork meat loin dry with clean paper towels; then generously brush with the oil
4. Scatter the spices and the nuts over a large rimmed baking sheet; then shake very well in order to create the same level of spices
5. Roll the pork loin into your prepared spices and set aside the spices to create an even layer.
6. Fill the water pan with cold water and place the pork in the gas smoker
7. Close the lid of the gas smoker and smoke the pork for about 4 hours or until the thermometer reads about 145° F for the internal temperature of the meat
8. Set the pork loin aside to rest for about 10 to 15 minutes
9. Slice the pork loin; then serve and enjoy it!

NUTRITION INFORMATION

Calories: 169, Fat: 5.7g, Carbohydrates: 2.6g, Dietary Fiber: 0.6 g, Protein: 25.8g

PULLED PORK

(Prep time: 12 Hours|Cook Time: 8 Hours| Ser vings: 7)

INGREDIENTS

- 1 Pork shoulder of about 6 to 8 pounds
- For the rub:
- 5 Tablespoons of white sugar
- 5 Tablespoons of light brown sugar
- 2 Tablespoons of kosher salt
- 2 Tablespoons of paprika
- 1 Tablespoon of onion powder
- 1 Tablespoon of freshly ground black pepper

- 1 Tablespoon of garlic powder
- 1 Medium chopped onion
- 3 Cups of hickory chips

INSTRUCTIONS

1. Start by placing the pork shoulder in a large pot; then add enough quantity of apple cider to cover it
2. Combine the white sugar with the paprika, the brown sugar, the salt, the paprika, the onion powder, the black pepper and the garlic powder in a large bowl and mix very well
3. Combine about ¼ cup of sugar rub into the cider and reserve the remaining rub; then cover the pot and refrigerate for about 12 hours.
4. Prepare your gas smoker by preheating it to about 210 degrees F; then add enough wood chips to the smoker box
5. Pour the cider brine into the water pan of the gas smoker
6. Add the onion with about ¼ cup or more of sugar rub
7. Spread the remaining quantity of rub over the pork shoulder and transfer the pork to the centre of the smoker
8. Smoke the pork shoulder for about 8 hours and you can add ore hickory chips and water as needed
9. Just 30 minutes before shredding the pork meat, transfer the pork to a platter and let cool for 30 minutes
10. Shred the pork shoulder with two forks
11. Serve and enjoy your dish!

NUTRITION INFORMATION

Calories: 220.1, Fat: 15.4g, Carbohydrates: 1g, Dietary Fiber: 0.3 g, Protein: 20g

SMOKED PORK SAUSAGE

(Prep time: 4 Hours|Cook Time: 6 Hours| Servings: 9-10)

INGREDIENTS

- 5 lbs of fresh ham or pork shoulder
- 2 Tablespoons of garlic powder
- 3 Teaspoons of salt
- 3 Teaspoons of ground black pepper
- 2 Teaspoon of dried marjoram
- 1 Cup of cold water
- ½ Cup of skim milk powder
- 1 Teaspoons of cure sausage casings

INSTRUCTIONS

1. Chop the pork meat and the pork fat into cubes of about 1 to 2 inches each
2. Pass the pork through a meat grinder; and reserve about 1/3 of the quantity of the pork meat aside; then dice into small chunks
3. In a large mixing bowl, combine the meat with the garlic powder, the salt, the black pepper, the marjoram, the milk powder and the sausage casings; then combine thoroughly
4. Place the pork meat in the refrigerator for about 4 hours or so
5. Remove the mixture of the meat from the refrigerator and stuff your sausages according to the instructions of the sausage stuffer
6. Soak cherry wood chips in water for about 30 minutes
7. Fill the smoker box with the already soaked wood chips; then pour cold water in the water pan
8. Preheat your gas smoker for about 25 minutes at a temperature of 170°F
9. Place the sausages in your gas smoker and smoker for about 2 hours; then increase the temperature to 190° F and smoke the sausages for about 3 hours
10. When the time is up, remove the sausages from the gas smoker and place it into a hot water bath for about 45 minutes
11. Remove the sausages from the water bath and hang it for about 2 hours
12. Serve and enjoy your sausages!

NUTRITION INFORMATION

Calories: 170, Fat: 13g, Carbohydrates: 1g, Dietary Fiber: 1 g, Protein: 11g

SMOKED SHORT PORK RIBS

(Prep time: 1Hour|Cook Time: 4 Hours| Servings: 4)

INGREDIENTS

- 2 lbs of baby back ribs; about 2 slabs
- ½ Cup of brown sugar
- ¼ Cup of smoked paprika
- 1 and ½ tablespoons of kosher salt
- 1 Tablespoon of ground black pepper
- 2 Teaspoons of garlic powder
- 2 Teaspoons of onion powder
- ½ Teaspoon of cayenne pepper
- The Basting liquid of wine vinegar; apple juice or red wine
- Water for the gas smoker
- Apple wood chips

INSTRUCTIONS

1. Soak the wood chips in a bowl for about 30 minutes
2. Start by laying the ribs flat on top of a clean surface with the meat side down
3. Remove the membrane so that you can be able to grab the end of the cut with a paper towel
4. Remove the membrane of the meat cuts and to do that just slice it at one of the ends with a paring knife; then use the paper towel to grab the end with it and peel the layer of the membrane
5. Combine all the dry rub ingredients in a medium bowl; then sprinkle the mixture rub on the top of the meat; in the bottom and the sides of the meat ribs
6. Let the ribs aside to rest for about 30 minutes
7. Preheat your gas smoker to a temperature of about 225° F
8. Add a small quantity of water to the pan in your gas smoker in order to keep the ribs moist
9. Fill the drawer with soaked wood chips

10. Place the rib with the meat side up on top of the smoker rack and cook in your smoker for about 3 hours; meanwhile prepare the sauce while the ribs are being smoked
11. After about 3 hours, place about 2 large sheets of heavy-duty aluminium foil on top of a flat surface.
12. Place a rack of pork ribs on each sheet of foil; then baste with the liquid you have; then wrap the ribs in the foil
13. Place the wrapped ribs in the gas smoker once again and cook for about 1 and ½ hours
14. Serve and enjoy your delicious dish!

NUTRITION INFORMATION

15. Calories: 170, Fat: 13g, Carbohydrates: 1g, Dietary Fiber: 1 g, Protein: 11g

SMOKED PORK WITH APPLE COMPOTE

(Prep time: 60 Minutes|Cook Time: 2 Hours| Servings: 4)

INGREDIENTS

- 4 Boneless pork chops of about 1 inch of thickness
- 1 Cup of your favourite BBQ rub
- For The Apple Compote
- 1 Tablespoon of canola oil
- 2 Tablespoons of water
- 1 Spanish onion
- 2 Granny smith tart apples
- 2 Tablespoons of butter

- ¼ Teaspoon of cinnamon
- ¼ Teaspoon of dry mustard
- ¼ Teaspoon of nutmeg
- 1 Pinch of salt

INSTRUCTIONS

1. Soak apple wood chips into water for about 40 minutes
2. Fill the smoke box with the soaked apple wood chips and preheat the Gas smoker for about 40 minutes
3. While your smoker is being preheated, season the pork chops with the BBQ rub
4. Place a baking rack over the top and place the pork chops on top of it
5. When the smoker is being preheated, set your smoker to a temperature of 225 degrees Fahrenheit.
6. Insert the digital thermometer into the thickest part of the pork chop and when the temperature indicates 145° F; place the baking sheet with the rack into a smoker
7. Smoke the pork chops for about 40 minutes; then make the compote
8. Thinly slice the onion; then add the oil to a skillet over a low heat
9. Add the onion to the skillet and cook for about 30 minutes
10. Remove the onion from the skillet and set it aside
11. Remove the skin of the apples and cut into pieces of ½ inch each
12. Melt the butter in the same skillet used for the onions and add the cinnamon, the apples, the dry mustard and the nutmeg
13. Sauté your ingredients until the apples become soft, then add in the onion back to the skillet and ix a little bit to combine
14. Season the compote with salt
15. Serve and enjoy your delicious smoked pork with the apple compote!

NUTRITION INFORMATION

Calories: 252.6, Fat: 9.4g, Carbohydrates: 9.2g, Dietary Fiber: 1.5 g, Protein: 31.5g

CHAPTER 4: GAS SMOKER LAMB RECIPES

SMOKED LAMB LOIN

(Prep time: 3 Hours|Cook Time: 4 Hours| Servings: 5-6)

INGREDIENTS

- 2 Pounds of boned rolled lamb loin
- 4 Halved garlic cloves
- 8 Fresh rosemary sprigs
- 1 Teaspoon of dried chilli flakes
- 1 Tablespoon of olive oil
- 2 Handfuls of apple wood chips

INSTRUCTIONS

1. Start by placing the lamb loin in a large baking dish and pierce the lamb into about 8 places with a sharp knife; then push the garlic and the rosemary into the cuts you have made
2. Sprinkle the lamb with the chilli in large shallow baking dish and rub it with oil: then cover and let refrigerate for about 3 hours or for an overnight
3. Soak the smoking chips into a large bowl filled with water for about 2 hours; then drain it very well
4. Place the drained smoking chips in the smoke box and fill the smoke pan with water
5. Place the lamb loin on a rack in your gas smoker and lock the lid
6. Smoke the lamb for about 3 to 4 Hours at a temperature of 225° F
7. When the time is up; check the inner temperature of the meat and when it indicates 160° F turn off the smoker
8. Remove the lamb from the gas smoker and set aside for about 10 minutes to cool down
9. Slice the smoked lamb; then serve and enjoy it!

NUTRITION INFORMATION

Calories: 171.5, Fat: 7.9g, Carbohydrates: 0.4g, Dietary Fiber: 0.1 g, Protein: 23.3g

SMOKED LAMB SHOULDER
(Prep time: 30 Minutes|Cook Time: 3-4 Hours| Servings: 8)

INGREDIENTS

- 4 to 8lb of Lamb shoulder
- 2 Tablespoons of Olive oil
- For the herb rub:
- 2 Tablespoons of salt
- 1 Tablespoon of dried parsley
- 2 Tablespoons of dried crushed sage
- 1 Tablespoon of dried rosemary
- 1 Tablespoon of dried thyme

- 1 Tablespoon of dried oregano
- 1 Tablespoon of dried basil
- 1 Tablespoon of dried crushed bay leaf
- 1 Tablespoon of ground black pepper
- 1 Tablespoon of sugar
- 2 Handfuls of cherry woodchips

INSTRUCTIONS

1. Soak the wood chips into a large bowl filled with water for about 30 minutes
2. Place the soaked chips in the smoke box and fill the smoke pan with water
3. Heat the gas smoker for about 30 minutes at a temperature of 190° F
4. Mix the dried parsley with the dried crushed sage, the dried rosemary, the dried thyme, the dried oregano, the dried basil, the dried crushed bay leaf, the ground black pepper and the sugar in a large bowl and mix very well
5. Coat the lamb shoulder very well into the olive oil; then sprinkle the salt over the lamb evenly
6. Apply the herb rub to the lamb meat making sure that it covers it evenly
7. Place the seasoned lamb shoulder with the fat side up on a rack in your preheated gas smoker
8. Close the door of the gas smoker and smoke the lamb shoulder for about 3 to 4 hours at a temperature of 225°F
9. Remove the lamb from the gas smoker when the internal temperature reaches about 195° F and wrap it in aluminium foil; then let rest for about 10 minutes
10. Slice the lamb; then serve and enjoy it with your favourite sauce!

NUTRITION INFORMATION

Calories: 285, Fat: 19.3g, Carbohydrates: 0.3g, Dietary Fiber: 0 g, Protein: 26.4g

Smoked Leg Of Lamb

(Prep time: 40 Minutes|Cook Time: 4 Hours| Servings: 4)

INGREDIENTS

- 1 Tablespoon of kosher salt
- 2 Teaspoons of black pepper
- 1 Teaspoon of granulated garlic
- 1 Teaspoon of thyme
- 1 Teaspoon of rosemary
- 1 Teaspoon of brown sugar
- ½ Teaspoon of paprika
- For the Lamb:

- 1 Leg of lamb, bone in
- 2 Tablespoons of yellow mustard
- 2 Handfuls of fruit wood chips

INSTRUCTIONS

1. Soak the wood chips in a large bowl filled with water and set it aside for about 40 minutes
2. Place the wood chips in the smoke box and fill the smoker pan with water
3. Heat the gas smoker at a temperature of about 130° F for 20 minutes
4. Combine the salt with the pepper, the garlic, the thyme, the rosemary, the sugar and the paprika in a bowl and mix very well
5. Check the lamb and remove any pieces of fat from it; then apply a thin layer of mustard on top of the lamb and sprinkle with the herb rub in one even layer on top of the meat
6. Place the lamb over the rack in your smoker and smoke for about 4 hours at a temperature of 225°F
7. When the internal temperature of the meat indicates 65° C/ 150° F, remove the meat from the gas smoker and set aside to cool for about 5 to 10 minutes
8. Serve and enjoy your dish!

NUTRITION INFORMATION

Calories: 165, Fat: 15g, Carbohydrates: 4g, Dietary Fiber: 1 g, Protein: 18g

PULLED LAMB

(Prep time: 35 Minutes|Cook Time: 10 Hours| Servings: 4-5)

INGREDIENTS

- 1 Lamb shoulder
- 1 Bunch of fresh rosemary
- 1 Bunch of fresh mint baste
- 1 Cup of apple cider vinegar
- 1 Cup of water
- 1 Can of dark beer
- ¼ Cup of Worcestershire sauce
- 1 Tablespoon of chopped rosemary

- 1 Tablespoon of dark brown sugar
- ½ Tablespoon of salt
- ½ Tablespoon of crushed fresh garlic
- 1 Teaspoon of hot smoked paprika
- Fruitwood wood chips such like Apple
- 1 Handful of fresh rosemary

INSTRUCTIONS

1. Soak the wood chips into a bowl filled with water for about 15 to 20 minutes
2. Combine the mint with the cider vinegar, the water, the dark beer, the Worcestershire sauce, the brown sugar, the garlic and the paprika in a saucepan and stir over a low heat and let simmer for about 5 minutes
3. Remove about ¾ of the simmered baste from the saucepan and let cool
4. Heat the remaining quantity of baste and let boil; then add 1 other tablespoon of brown sugar to the baste and mix
5. Place the wood chips in the smoker box and preheat the gas smoker to a low temperature of 105° C 220° F for about 15 minutes
6. Place the lamb in your gas smoker and smoke it for about 8 to 10 hours
7. Baste the lamb shoulder once per hour; and when the temperature reaches 90° C 195° F
8. Remove the lamb from the smoker; then place the lamb on a double layer of aluminium foil and add 1 bunch of rosemary and dried mint
9. Reheat the baste and add 1 tablespoon of sugar to it; then let the lamb rest for about 25 minutes
10. Shred the meat with a fork; then serve and enjoy it with the cooked dip!

NUTRITION INFORMATION

Calories: 238.9, Fat: 17.4g, Carbohydrates: 0g, Dietary Fiber: 0.2 g, Protein: 18.8g

SMOKED LAMB MEATBALLS

(Prep time: 20 Minutes|Cook Time: 1 Hour| Servings: 12)

INGREDIENTS

FOR THE MEATBALLS

- 1 Pound of ground lamb shoulder
- 3 Finely diced garlic cloves
- 3 Tablespoons of diced onion or shallot
- 1 Teaspoon of salt
- 1 Large egg
- ½ Teaspoon of pepper

- ½ Teaspoon of cumin
- ½ Teaspoon of smoked paprika
- ¼ Teaspoon of red pepper flakes
- ¼ Teaspoon of ground cinnamon
- ¼ Cup of Panko breadcrumbs
- 1 Handful of cherry wood chips

INSTRUCTIONS

1. Soak the wood chips in a bowl filled with water for about 20 minutes
2. Fill the smoker box with cherry wood chips and fill the smoker pan with water
3. Preheat your gas smoker to a temperature of 225° F
4. In a large bowl, combine the ground lamb with the garlic, the diced onion, the salt, the egg, the pepper, the cumin, the smoked paprika, the cinnamon, the red pepper flakes and the Panko bread
5. Mix the ingredients with your hands very well; then form small balls; then place the balls over a baking sheet
6. Place the baking sheet with the meatballs over a rack in your gas smoker and close the door
7. Set the temperature at about 225° F and smoke the meatballs for about 1 to 1 and ½ hours or until the internal temperature of the meatballs reaches about 160°F
8. Remove the baking sheet with the meatballs on top of it and serve it immediately
9. Enjoy your dish!

NUTRITION INFORMATION

Calories: 219.5, Fat: 8.7g, Carbohydrates: 15.6g, Dietary Fiber: 0.4 g, Protein: 20.4g

CHAPTER 5: GAS SMOKER CHICKEN RECIPES

SMOKED WHOLE CHICKEN

(Prep time: 24 Hours|Cook Time: 2 Hours| Servings: 6)

INGREDIENTS

- 1 Chicken, whole
- 2 ½ litres of water
- 2 Tablespoon of salt
- 1 Tablespoon of honey
- 1 Teaspoon of ground pepper
- 1 Tablespoon of oil
- 2 Handfuls of apple wood chips

INSTRUCTIONS

1. Combine the water with the salt, the honey and the pepper in a large pan to make the mixture brine
2. Remove the chicken backbone and flatten it; then submerge it into the prepared brine and refrigerate for about 24 hours
3. Place the wood chips in the smoker box and fill the water pan with cold water
4. Pre-heat your Gas smoker to about 110°C, 225° F
5. Drain the chicken and pour the boiling water over the top of the skin
6. Pat the whole chicken dry with clean paper towels and rub it with oil.
7. Place the chicken in your smoker at a temperature of about 110°C, 225° F and smoker for about 2 hours
8. Let the chicken rest for about 10 minutes
9. Serve and enjoy your dish!

NUTRITION INFORMATION

Calories: 264, Fat: 15.2g, Carbohydrates: 0g, Dietary Fiber: 0.4 g, Protein: 29g

CHICKEN LEGS WITH ORANGE SAUCE

(Prep time: 8 Hours|Cook Time: 4 Hours| Servings: 6)

INGREDIENTS

- 6 Chicken leg quarters about 5 and ½ pounds 1/3 Cup of olive oil
- 1 Tablespoon of loosely packed orange zest
- 1 Tablespoon of loosely packed lime zest
- 1/3 Cup of fresh orange juice
- ¼ Cup of fresh lime juice
- 1 Bunch of fresh cilantro with the stems removed
- 6 Garlic large cloves
- 2 Seeded, red jalapeño peppers
- ¼ Cup of fresh oregano leaves
- 1 and ¼ teaspoons of ground cumin
- 1 Teaspoon of kosher salt
- ½ Teaspoon of black pepper
- 3 Cups of apple wood chips

INSTRUCTIONS

1. Pulse the olive oil, the orange zest, the lime zest, the orange juice, the lime juice, the cilantro, the garlic cloves, the red peppers, the oregano leaves, the ground cumin and the kosher salt for about 20 seconds
2. Reserve the mixture and reserve ½ cup of the mixture for using it later
3. Place the chicken in a bowl and add the remaining mixture; then toss very well and refrigerate the mixture for about 4 to 8 hours
4. Place about 3 cups of dry apple wood chips in centre of the smoker box
5. Preheat your gas smoker to a temperature of about 225° F for about 5 minutes
6. Pat the chicken dry with clean paper towels and leave the marinade on the skin
7. Sprinkle the chicken with salt and pepper
8. Place the chicken over a rack in your gas smoker; then smoke the chicken for about 3 to 4 hours

9. Check the inner temperature of the chicken legs and make sure it is about 165° F
10. Transfer the chicken to a serving platter
11. Serve and enjoy your chicken legs with the sauce!

NUTRITION INFORMATION

Calories: 257, Fat: 15.4g, Carbohydrates: 0g, Dietary Fiber: 0 g, Protein: 28.4g

PROSCIUTTO WRAPPED CHICKEN BREAST

(Prep time: 1 Hour|Cook Time: 2 Hours| Servings: 4)

INGREDIENTS

- 2 ½ Pound of Chicken breasts
- Slices of Prosciutto
- 1 ¼ cups of Pesto spread
- 3 Cups of apple wood chips

INSTRUCTIONS

1. Place the apple wood chips in the smoker box and preheat your Gas smoker at a temperature of 220° F for about 15 minutes
2. Spread the pesto on top of the chicken breast and wrap the slices of Prosciutto on top of the chicken breast
3. Secure the chicken breast with a toothpick
4. Place the chicken on a rack in your gas smoker and add an additional handful of wood chips to the smoker box
5. Smoke the chicken breast for about 2 hours on LOW 105 to 135° F, 220-275° F
6. Serve and enjoy your smoked chicken breasts!

NUTRITION INFORMATION

Calories: 233, Fat: 14g, Carbohydrates: 3g, Dietary Fiber: 0 g, Protein: 23g

CHAPTER 6: GAS SMOKER TURKEY RECIPES

SMOKED TURKEY

(Prep time: 15 Minutes|Cook Time: 10 Hours|
Servings: 5)

INGREDIENTS

- 1 Turkey with the neck and giblets removed
- 2 Tablespoons of salt
- 4 Crushed garlic cloves
- ½ Cup of butter
- 1 Chopped apple
- 1 Tablespoon of garlic powder
- 1 Medium, chopped onion
- 1 Can of soft drink
- 1 Tablespoon of ground black pepper

INSTRUCTIONS

1. Preheat your Gas Smoker to a temperature of about 110° C, 225° F
2. Rinse the turkey under cold water and pat it dry with paper towels
3. Rub the garlic over the turkey and sprinkle with the seasoned salt
4. Place the turkey in a roasting pan and fill its cavity with the butter, the soft drink, the apple, the onion, the garlic powder, the salt and the ground black pepper
5. Cover the turkey with the aluminium foil and place it in the gas smoker
6. Smoker the turkey at about 225° F for about 10 hours or until the internal temperature indicates 165° F; and make sure to baste every 2 hours
7. Serve and enjoy your turkey!

NUTRITION INFORMATION

Calories: 220, Fat: 18g, Carbohydrates: 0g, Dietary Fiber: 0 g, Protein: 34g

SMOKED TURKEY LEGS

(Prep time: 30 Minutes|Cook Time: 4-6 Hours| Servings: 7-8)

INGREDIENTS

FOR THE BRINE INGREDIENTS

- 7 to 8 turkey legs
- 1 Gallon of water
- 1 Cup of kosher salt
- ½ Cup of sugar
- 2 tablespoons of onion powder
- 2 tablespoons of chilli powder
- 1 tablespoon of garlic powder
- 1 tablespoon of paprika
- 1 tablespoon of ground pepper
- 1 teaspoon of ground cumin

FOR THE SEASONING

- 3 Tablespoon of onion powder
- 2 Tablespoon of paprika
- 1 Tablespoon of garlic powder
- 1 Teaspoon of ground pepper
- 1 Teaspoon of ground cumin
- 3 Tablespoons of vegetable or light olive oil
- 2 Handfuls of woodchips of your choice

INSTRUCTIONS

1. Start by mixing the water with the kosher salt , the sugar, the onion powder, the chilli powder, the garlic powder, the paprika, the ground pepper and the ground cumin in a large pan on the stove and bring the ingredients to a boil; then stir

2. Let the brine cool at room temperature; then add the turkey legs and mix

3. Place the turkey legs in the refrigerator for about 6 hours

4. Remove the turkey legs from the mixture of the brine and pat it dry

5. Mix the onion powder, the paprika, the garlic powder, the ground pepper, the cumin and the olive oil in a bowl and rub the outside of the turkey legs with the prepared rub

6. Place the wood chips in the smoker box and fill the smoker water pan with cool water; then preheat the smoker for about 10 minutes at about 225° F

7. Place the turkey legs over the rack in your Gas smoker and smoke it for about 4 to 6 hours or just until the inner temperature of the meat indicates 165° F

8. Let the meat rest for about 20 minutes

9. Serve and enjoy your turkey legs!

NUTRITION INFORMATION

Calories: 165, Fat: 14g, Carbohydrates: 0.5g, Dietary Fiber: 0 g, Protein: 15.2g

TURKEY WITH CRANBERRY SAUCE

(Prep time: 30 Minutes|Cook Time: 6 Hours| Servings: 6)

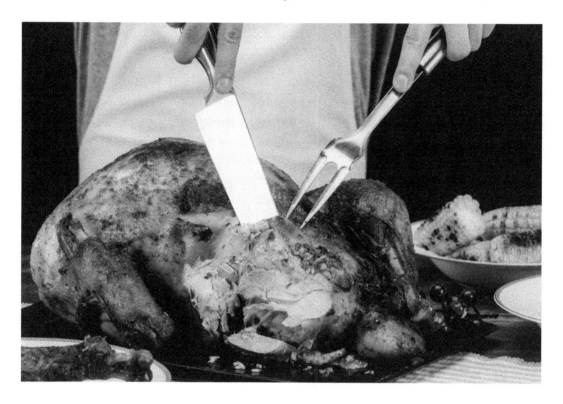

INGREDIENTS

- 5 Pounds of turkey
- For the seasoned butter:
- 1 Stick of softened unsalted butter
- The juice of half a lemon
- 1 Tablespoon of lemon zest
- 1Tablespoon of black pepper
- 1Finely minced garlic clove
- 2 Teaspoons of salt
- ½ Tablespoon of chopped fresh thyme

FOR THE CRANBERRY SAUCE

- ½ Tablespoon of orange zest
- 1 Cup of sugar
- 1 Cup of water
- 12 Ounces of cranberries
- 1 Pinch of ground cinnamon
- 1 Pinch of salt

EQUIPMENTS

2 Handfuls of apple wood chips

INSTRUCTIONS

1. Place the wood chips in the smoker box of the gas smoker and preheat your Gas smoker at a temperature of about 110° C/225° F
2. Remove the turkey neck and giblets; then rinse the turkey and pat it dry with clean paper towels
3. Whisk your ingredients very well together; then place the seasoned butter in a bowl
4. Loosen the turkey skin with your fingers and place 2 tablespoons of the seasoned butter under the skin of the turkey breast; then brush the remaining quantity on the outside part of the turkey
5. Place the turkey over a rack in your Gas smoker and add wood chips to the smoker box if needed
6. Smoke the turkey for about 4 to 6 hours or until the internal temperature reaches about 165° F
7. Pour the orange zest with the sugar, the water, the cranberries, the cinnamon, the salt, the1 Pinch of ground cinnamon in a medium saucepan over a medium high heat and add the salt
8. Let your ingredients boil for about 15 minutes; then remove the turkey from the oven and let rest for 10 minutes
9. Serve the turkey with the cranberry sauce and enjoy its heavenly taste!

NUTRITION INFORMATION

Calories: 259.2, Fat: 14g, Carbohydrates: 29g, Dietary Fiber: 1.5 g, Protein: 36.5g

CHAPTER 7: GAS SMOKER FISH RECIPES

SMOKED TROUT

(Prep time: 24 Hours|Cook Time: 4 Hours| Servings: 7)

INGREDIENTS

- 7 Cleaned and rinsed whole trout of 10 inches each
- 4 Cups of water
- ½ Cup of sugar
- ½ Cup of non iodized salt
- 2 Tablespoons of chilli powder
- 2 Tablespoons of garlic powder
- 3 Bamboo skewers, chopped into pieces of 3 inches each
- Melted butter

INSTRUCTIONS

1. Mix the sugar, the salt, the chilli, the garlic, the water and the butter in a large bowl and place the trout into the mixture
2. Cover the trout and let marinate for an overnight in the refrigerator
3. Remove the trout from the refrigerator and pat it dry with paper towels
4. Put the trout fillets between two layers of clean paper towels and set aside for about 30 minutes
5. Preheat your Gas smoker for about 10 minutes on LOW
6. Put the bamboo skewer at its length in an horizontal way inside each of the trout to hold it open
7. Smoke the trout on LOW, at about 110° C/225° F for about 3 to 4 hours
8. Replace the wood chips twice or thrice
9. Smoke the trout on Low for about 3 to 4 hours.
10. If you want more flavour, you can glaze each of the fillets whenever you replace woodchips or water to the water bowl
11. Serve and enjoy your dish!

NUTRITION INFORMATION

Calories: 110.1, Fat: 6.1g, Carbohydrates: 0g, Dietary Fiber: 0 g, Protein: 13.8g

GLAZED SALMON WITH LEMON SLICES

(Prep time: 24 Hours|Cook Time: 1 Hour| Servings: 4)

INGREDIENTS

- 3 Salmon fillet portions with the skin removed
- Slices of Lemon

FOR THE GLAZE

- ⅓ Cup of olive oil
- 1½ Tablespoons of apple cider vinegar
- ⅓ Cup of soy sauce
- ¼ Cup of chopped spring onions
- 1 Tablespoon of grated fresh ginger
- 1 Teaspoon of minced garlic
- Pre-soaked Cedar planks
- 3 Handful of woodchips and herbs

INSTRUCTIONS

1. Start by soaking the Cedar planks into water for an overnight
2. Combine the olive oil with the apple cider vinegar, the soy sauce, the chopped onions; the ginger and the garlic and mix very well
3. Place the salmon fillets into the glaze and let marinate for about an hour
4. Preheat the gas smoker to a medium temperature of about 135-160°C 275 to 320°F
5. Also, preheat the planks in the smoker
6. Drain the salmon and drain it very well; then place it over the planks and place a lemon slice on top of each one
7. Smoke the Salmon for about 1 hour
8. When the internal temperature reaches 60° C/ 115°F
9. Serve and enjoy your dish!

NUTRITION INFORMATION

Calories: 120, Fat: 6g, Carbohydrates: 0g, Dietary Fiber: 0 g, Protein: 15g

SMOKED MACKEREL

(Prep time: 2 Hours|Cook Time: 1 Hour| Servings: 3)

INGREDIENTS

- 4 mackerels
- 2 litres of water or ½ gallon
- 1 lb of non-iodized salt

INSTRUCTIONS

1. Start by making the brine and to do that mix the salt and the water; you will need heat to dissolve the salt with water
2. Transfer the brine to a bucket; then when it cools completely; immerse the mackerel in it for about 1 and ½ hours
3. It is compulsory to fully immerse the mackerel into the water
4. After brining the mackerel; rinse it very well with fresh water; then hang it for an overnight to dry in a cool place
5. Turn on your gas smoker to a temperature of about 40° C; 95° F
6. Cold smoke the mackerel for about 4 hours; then hot smoke it for about 2 additional hours at a temperature of about 200°F
7. Turn the gas on and off intermittently but ensuring that the temperature ideally hovered between 30°C and 40°C (around 100°F).
8. Cold smoke for 4 hours and then hot smoke for 2 additional hours at a temperature of about 200° F

NUTRITION INFORMATION

Calories: 293, Fat: 23.5g, Carbohydrates: 0g, Dietary Fiber: 0.2 g, Protein: 20g

CHAPTER 8: GAS SMOKER SEAFOOD RECIPES

SMOKED SHRIMP

(Prep time: 30 Minutes|Cook Time: 1 Hour| Servings: 3)

INGREDIENTS

FOR THE SHRIMP

- 1 Pound of peeled and deveined shrimp
- 1 Tablespoon of sesame oil
- 1 Tablespoon minced ginger
- 4 Tablespoons of honey
- 6 Tablespoons of sriracha
- 2 Tablespoons of lime juice
- 3 Handfuls of fruit wood chips

INSTRUCTIONS

1. Combine the sesame oil with the ginger, the honey, the sriracha and the lime juice in a large bowl.
2. Reserve about half of the marinade and add the shrimp to the other remaining half; then mix until the shrimp become evenly coated.
3. Place the wood chips in your gas smoker box and fill the smoker bowl with water
4. Preheat your gas smoker for about 15 minutes at about 225° F
5. Once the gas smoker is preheated; arrange the shrimps on the rack in your gas smoker and smoke it for about 1 hour
6. Coat the shrimp with the remaining honey sriracha; then remove the shrimp from the gas smoker
7. Serve and enjoy the delicious taste!

NUTRITION INFORMATION

Calories: 100, Fat: 4g, Carbohydrates: 0g, Dietary Fiber: 0.3 g, Protein: 10g

SMOKED OYSTERS

(Prep time: 10 Minutes|Cook Time: 1 Hour| Servings: 4)

INGREDIENTS

- 1½ Pounds of oysters
- 3 Garlic cloves
- 1 Pinch of ground black pepper
- 2 Handfuls of Light wood chips

INSTRUCTIONS

1   Preheat your Gas smoker to a temperature of about 90° C/ 195° F
2   Bring a large pan of water to a boil; then remove the oysters from the shells and reserve the liquor aside
3   Toss the oysters into the boiled water; then stir it into water and blanch for about 5 to 6 seconds
4   Fill the smoker box with the wood chips and fill the smoker bowl with water
5   Place an aluminium foil over the rack in your gas smoker
6   Remove the oysters from the water and place the oysters over the rack, lined with aluminium foil in the smoker
7   Smoke the oysters for about 1 hour at a temperature of about 225° F
8   Once the oysters are smoked, remove the oysters from your gas smoker and set the oysters to cool for 10 minutes
9   Serve and enjoy the oysters with olive oil!

NUTRITION INFORMATION

Calories: 170, Fat: 10g, Carbohydrates: 8g, Dietary Fiber: 1 g, Protein: 14g

SMOKED CRAB LEGS

(Prep time: 10 Minutes|Cook Time: 30 Minutes| Servings: 11)

INGREDIENTS

- 10lbs of Snow Crab Legs
- 1lb of Butter
- 2 Tablespoons of BBQ Rub
- 1 Tablespoon of dried Parsley
- ½ Teaspoon of Crab/Shrimp Boil seasoning
- The juice of 1 lemon
- The drawn butter
- A few lemon slices

- 1 Cup of cocktail sauce
- 3 Handfuls of apple wood chips

INSTRUCTIONS

1. Prepare your gas smoker by placing the wood chips on the smoker box
2. Preheat the gas smoker for about 10 minutes at a temperature of 225° F
3. Melt the butter in a saucepan over a low heat; then add the BBQ Rub, the crab and shrimp boil seasoning, the parsley and the lemon juice and mix very well
4. Add 1 handful of seasoned wood chips to the smoker box and fill the smoker bowl with water
5. Put the butter mixture into an aluminium steam pan;; then dredge each of the crab legs into the butter and reserve the remaining mixture for basting
6. Arrange the crab clusters over a rack in your gas smoker and close the lid
7. Smoke the crab clusters for about 30 minutes at a temperature of about 225° F
8. Remove the crab legs from the smoker when the time is up
9. Serve the crab clusters from the smoker and serve it immediately
10. Enjoy your delicious seafood dish with lime wedges!

NUTRITION INFORMATION

Calories: 300, Fat: 4g, Carbohydrates: 0g, Dietary Fiber: 1 g, Protein: 56g

CHAPTER 9: GAS SMOKER GAME AND RABBIT RECIPES

SMOKED DUCK BREAST

(Prep time: 24 Hours|Cook Time: 3 Hours| Servings: 3)

INGREDIENTS

- 3 Duck breasts
- 1 Pint of apple juice
- 2 Teaspoons of salt
- 1 to 2 bay leaves
- 2 Teaspoons of dried thyme
- 1 Teaspoon of Salt Petre
- 3 Cups of plum or orange wood chips

INSTRUCTIONS

1 Remove the breasts of the duck from the bones; then trim any fat from the duck breast
2 Mix the apple juice, the salt, the bay leaves, the dry thyme and the salt in a medium bowl and mix very well
3 Mix your ingredients and pop the duck breasts the prepared brine; then cover the breasts and refrigerate for an overnight
4 Remove the duck breasts from the refrigerator and from the brine and hang it to dry very well for about 1 hour
5 Fill the smoker box of your gas smoker with the apple wood chips
6 Place the duck breasts over a rack in your gas smoker
7 Smoke the duck breasts for about 3 hours at a temperature of about 63° C/145° F
8 When the smoking process is finished; let the duck breast cool for about 10 to 15 minutes
9 Slice the smoked duck breasts; then serve and enjoy your dish!

NUTRITION INFORMATION

Calories: 239, Fat: 39g, Carbohydrates: 0g, Dietary Fiber: 1.3 g, Protein: 11g

SMOKED RABBIT

(Prep time: 1 Hour|Cook Time: 4 Hours| Servings: 5)

INGREDIENTS

- Skinned and gutted cottontail
- 2 Tablespoons of kosher salt
- ½ Cup of white vinegar
- 1 Cup of water
- For the Rub:
- 1 Tablespoon of garlic powder
- 1 Tablespoon of cayenne pepper
- 1 Tablespoon of salt
- 1 Tablespoon of black pepper
- 1 Bottle of barbecue sauce
- 2 Cups of lemon wood chips

INSTRUCTIONS

1 Start by making the brine by dissolving the salt into the white vinegar
2 Pour the prepared brine on top of the rabbit in a large and shallow dish; then pour in water to cover the rabbit
3 Set the rabbit aside for about 1 hour
4 Place the wood chips in your smoker box and fill the smoker pan with water
5 Preheat your gas smoker to a temperature of 200° F
6 Remove the rabbit from the brine and pat it dry very well; then mix the garlic powder with the cayenne pepper, the salt and the pepper and combine very well
7 Heavily season the rabbit with the prepared rub; then place the rabbit in the gas smoker and add more wood to the smoke box
8 Next, season the rabbit heavily with the prepared rub.
9 Place the rabbit in the gas smoker and smoke it for about 3 to 4 hours at a temperature of 225° F
10 Remove the rabbit from the gas smoker; then pour more BBQ sauce on top of the rabbit
11 Serve and enjoy your smoked rabbit!

NUTRITION INFORMATION

Calories: 239, Fat: 39g, Carbohydrates: 0g, Dietary Fiber: 1.3 g, Protein: 11g

SMOKED VENISON PATTIES

(Prep time: 30 Minutes|Cook Time: 1 Hour| Servings: 7)

INGREDIENTS

- ½lb of ground venison
- 4Oz ground of pork fat
- 1 Small, peeled and finely chopped onion
- 2 Tablespoons of redcurrant jelly
- 8 Tablespoons of breadcrumbs
- ¾ Teaspoon of salt
- ¼ Teaspoon of ground black pepper
- 2 Cups of lemon wood chips

INSTRUCTIONS

1   Place the ground venison, the ground pork fat, the peeled and chopped onion, the jelly, the breadcrumbs, the salt and pepper in a large bowl and mix very well
2   Form small patties from the mixture; then cover it with a wrap and refrigerate for about 30 minutes
3   Place the wood chips in the smoke box of your gas smoker and fill the smoke water bowl with cold water
4   Preheat your gas smoker for about 10 minutes at a temperature of 220°F
5   Remove the patties from the refrigerator and arrange it over the rack in your Gas smoker
6   Smoke the patties for about 60 minutes at a temperature of about 220° F
7   Serve and enjoy your smoked patties with your favourite BBQ sauce!

NUTRITION INFORMATION

Calories: 132, Fat: 2.7g, Carbohydrates: 0g, Dietary Fiber: 1g, Protein: 25.6g

SMOKED VENISON

(Prep time: 24 Hours|Cook Time: 6 Hours| Servings: 4)

INGREDIENTS

- 1 Venison roast of about 5 pounds
- 0.8 Ounce of kosher salt
- 0.8 Ounce of sugar
- 3 Cups of plum or apple wood chips

INSTRUCTIONS

1 Combine the salt with the sugar together in a small bowl; then massage the mixture into the venison
2 Place the venison in a plastic bag or container and refrigerate it for about 24 hours
3 Place the wood chips in the smoker box and fill the bowl with water; the preheat your Gas smoker at a temperature of about 225° F
4 Remove the venison from the refrigerator and pat it dry with clean paper towels
5 Place the venison in your gas smoker and smoke it at a temperature of about 200° F for about 4 to 6 hours
6 When the time is up; check if the internal temperature reaches about 140° F
7 Set the venison aside to cool for 10 minutes
8 Serve and enjoy your dish!

NUTRITION INFORMATION

Calories: 219, Fat: 15g, Carbohydrates: 0.8g, Dietary Fiber: 0.3g, Protein: 30g

SMOKED RABBIT

(Prep time: 2 Hours|Cook Time: 4 Hours| Servings: 5)

INGREDIENTS

- 1 Whole rabbit of about 2 lbs
- 1 lb of lean turkey sausage
- 1 Cup of uncooked plain oatmeal
- 1 Chopped onion
- ½ Cup of chopped celery
- ½ Cup of chopped carrot
- ½ Cup of chopped mixed portabella mushrooms
- 1 Peeled, cored and chopped apple
- 1 Large egg

- 1 Cup of beef broth
- 1 to 2 bay leaves
- 2 Teaspoons of sage
- 2 Teaspoons of parsley
- 2 Teaspoons of rosemary
- 1 Dash off dried cranberries
- ½ Cup of white wine vinegar
- 2 Cups of apple wood chips

INSTRUCTIONS

1. Start by washing the rabbit with the white vinegar; then soak the rabbit into the salt and water for about 2 hours
2. Place the wood chips in your smoke box and fill the water pan with cold water
3. Preheat the gas smoker at a temperature of 135° F for about 10 minutes
4. Pat the rabbit dry with clean paper towels; then season the inside and the outside of the rabbit with salt and pepper
5. Combine the oatmeal with the sausage, the celery, the carrots, the mushrooms, the apple, the sage, the rosemary, the parsley, the onions and the cranberries in a large mixing bowl and combine very well
6. Stuff the rabbit with the prepared stuffing and tie it closed with a cooking twine
7. Place the stuffed rabbit over a rack in your gas smoker and surround it with a foil
8. Smoke the rabbit for about 4 hours
9. When the internal temperature of the rabbit meat reaches 165° F, remove the rabbit from the smoker and set it aside for 6 minutes
10. Serve and enjoy your delicious dish!

NUTRITION INFORMATION

Calories: 145.8, Fat: 7g, Carbohydrates: 15.7g, Dietary Fiber: 3.2g, Protein: 6.9g

CHAPTER 10: GAS SMOKER VEGETABLE RECIPES

MUSHROOMS WITH CREAM CHEESE

(Prep time: 10 Minutes|Cook Time: 45 Minutes|
Servings: 4)

INGREDIENTS

- 1 lb of Portabella mushrooms
- 2 Tablespoons of Worcestershire sauce
- 2 Tablespoons of melted butter
- 1 Pinch of salt
- 1 Pinch of pepper
- 2 Cups of light apple flavoured woodchips

INSTRUCTIONS

1. Preheat your gas smoker to a Low temperature of about 105 to 135°C 220 to 275°F.
2. Start by cleaning the mushrooms; then remove the stems of the mushrooms and remove the black gills with the help of a spoon
3. Melt the butter in a small pan and add to it the Worcestershire sauce.
4. Coat your cleaned mushrooms with the mixture of the butter and season it with 1 of salt and 1 pinch of pepper.
5. Place the mushrooms in your gas smoker and smoker it for about 45 minutes
6. Serve and enjoy your delicious mushrooms!

NUTRITION INFORMATION

Calories: 60, Fat: 3.6g, Carbohydrates: 3.1g, Dietary Fiber: 1g, Protein: 4g

SMOKED CORN ON THE COBS

(Prep time: 2 Hours|Cook Time: 60 Minutes| Servings: 10)

INGREDIENTS

- 10 Ears of corn with the husks on
- ½ Cup of olive oil
- 2 Tablespoons of onion powder
- 1 Tablespoon of sweet paprika
- 2 Tablespoons of brown sugar
- 1 Tablespoons of mild chilli powder
- 1 Teaspoon of salt
- 1 Bunch of finely chopped green onions

INSTRUCTIONS

1. Start by gently pulling the husks on each of the ears of corn; then remove the silk from the corn; but make sure not to remove the husks
2. Put the ears in a large pot filled with water and set it aside for a couple of hours
3. Combine the olive oil with the onion powder, the paprika, the brown sugar, the chilli powder, and the salt in a bowl
4. Remove the corn from the water and brush it with the mixture of oil
5. Now, pull the husks back over the corn and prepare your smoker
6. Smoker the ears of corn at a temperature of about 110° C/225° F for about 1 hour
7. When you are done smoking; remove the ears of corn from the smoker
8. Top with the green onions; then serve and enjoy your delicious smoked corn on the cobs!

NUTRITION INFORMATION

Calories: 58, Fat: 0.5g, Carbohydrates: 14g, Dietary Fiber: 1.8g, Protein: 14g

SMOKED STUFFED POTATOES

(Prep time: 30 Minutes|Cook Time: 25 Minutes| Servings: 4)

INGREDIENTS

- 4 Medium Potatoes
- 1 Cup of grated Mozzarella cheese
- ½ Cup of finely chopped capsicum
- 1 Tin of sweet corn kernels
- 1 Teaspoon of chilli flakes
- 2 Teaspoons of dried oregano

INSTRUCTIONS

1. Preheat your Gas smoker to a medium temperature of about 135°C/275°F
2. Wash your potatoes and boil it into water until it is about half way cooked
3. Remove the potatoes from the pan; then carefully cut the potatoes into half
4. Scoop the inside of the cooked potatoes without breaking its skin
5. Save the already scooped of the potatoes in a bowl
6. Finely chop the capsicum, the sweet corn kernels, the oregano and the chilli flakes and combine the mixture with the scooped potato
7. Season the mixture of the potatoes with a little bit of salt and gently stir the mixture to combine the seasoning very well
8. Add a pinch of salt and a little bit of oil in a shallow dish and brush the skin of the potato boats with the salted oil
9. Spoon the mixture of the potatoes into each of the potato boats and sprinkle with grated cheese and ground black pepper
10. Fill the smoke box with lemon wood chips and fill the water bowl with cold water
11. Place the stuffed potatoes in your gas smoker at a temperature of about 150° C/ 295° F
12. Smoke the potatoes for about 25 minutes
13. Remove the potatoes from the gas smoker
14. Serve and enjoy your delicious stuffed smoked potatoes!

NUTRITION INFORMATION

Calories: 225.1, Fat: 13.8g, Carbohydrates: 24g, Dietary Fiber: 4.2g, Protein: 2.6g

__CONCLUSION__

Complete Gas Smoker and Grill Cookbook

The ultimate how-to guide for your _GAS smoker_, use this complete guide to smoke all types of meat, fish, game and veggies. An essential cookbook for those who want to smoke meat without needing expert help from others. Offers detailed guidance obtained by years of smoking meat includes clear instructions and step-by-step directions for every recipe. The only guide you will ever need to professionally smoke a variety of food, including _beef, pork, chicken, fish and seafood, lamb, turkey, vegetable, rabbit and game_ recipes such as:

- _Japanese-Style Smoked Steak_
- _Smoked Pork Loin_
- _Smoked Lamb Meatballs_
- _Turkey With Cranberry Sauce_
- _Glazed Salmon With Lemon Slices_
- _Smoked Crab Legs_
- _Smoked Rabbit_
- _Smoked Duck Breast_
- _Mushrooms With Cream Cheese_

The book includes photographs of every finished meal, helpful tips and tricks on GAS SMOKERS, making BBQ and SMOKING MEAT to make your job easier. Gas smoker is a revolutionary smoking technique that comes to challenge conventional smokers like wood smokers. Not only gas smokers are easy to clean and to use, but it is also very practical.

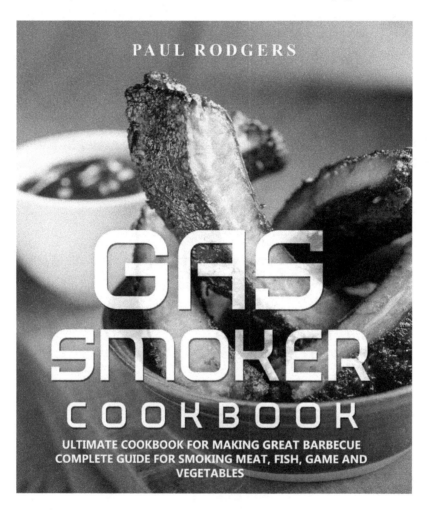

MY BOOKS

https://www.amazon.com/dp/B07L1DTWN8

https://www.amazon.com/dp/1797786385

GET YOUR FREE GIFT

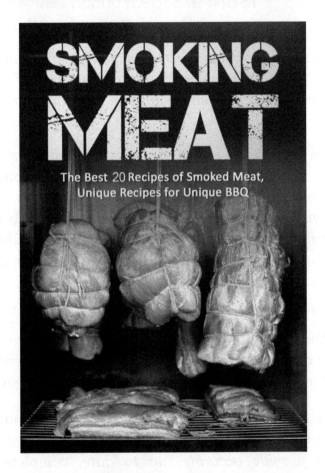

Subscribe to our Mail List and get your FREE copy of the book

'Smoking Meat: The Best 20 Recipes of Smoked Meat, Unique Recipes for Unique BBQ'

https://tiny.cc/smoke20